Eternal Love and Fear

Zachary Myers

ISBN: 978-1-4669-4091-8 (sc)
ISBN: 978-1-4669-4090-1 (e)

Trafford rev. 06/06/2012

 www.trafford.com

North America & international
toll-free: 1 888 232 4444 (USA & Canada)
phone: 250 383 6864 ♦ fax: 812 355 4082

For Dayna, the love of my life. Thank you for encouraging me to write and publish my poems. Thank you for believing in me, for being my muse and for being so kind and so very inspirational. I couldn't have done it without you. Thank you very much. I love you.

Hate and Madness

All this hate is maddening

And this fear is saddening

The darkness in me is frightening

All this emptiness makes everything seem unfulfilling

These thoughts are depressing

Life seems demeaning

I fear my life is nearly over

And I'll be the one losing

Dead Poet

I'm a dead poet

Nothing comes to me anymore

No inspiration, no motivation

Love is dead

Heart's about to burst

Filled my soul with sorrow and dread

That's not even the worst

But remember

Forever shall I love you

Always shall my words be true

But this is the last one

I'm forever done

Lost

You can see the hatred in my eyes

Darker than the fading of the night skies

Everything pure in me dies

I dare not tell any lies

For these are my last goodbyes

Concepts

The concept of reality is stability

Not only am I insane, but also mentally disturbed

My poems and riddles, full of solidity

Shows my future once deferred

Once I was scared of this

But now I'm full of bliss

Beyond Nightmares

Beyond the nightmares I draw a blank

Can't think of anything to write down

To the bottom of the abyss my heart sank

To my knees I fell, not making a sound

My body began to burn

Darkness making me drown

I think I'm going down

But it can't possibly be my turn

Conflict

Across the end of this conflict

I can see a slant to the free

I hear them

Hear them chanting for me

This hate I have, I feel like an addict

Cut

A razor to cut

I just can't seem to stop

Help me, I'm stuck in a rut

Losing my mind

To my knees I drop

Hold on, stop time

We're crossing the line

The world, burning for its crime

This kingdom of darkness is all mine

Sorrow

I'm filled with sorrow and dread

Might as well let them cut off my head

Or maybe slit my wrist and die in bed

I'm as good as dead

There is nothing left to be said

Mislead

I loved what you said to me so I wrote it down.

But when I gave you my heart, you struck it and

threw it to the ground. There's hate in these words and

hate in these eyes. I can't wait til everyone dies.

Scream

I want people to scream and die

They'll watch my anger burn up the sky

My hurt and pain is all that will remain

All the hate and abuse drove me insane

Love, hope, and dreams will fade away

Only misery, fear, and pain will stay

Pain

A world with no love and too much hate

My heart burst with a sharp pain

This was to be my fate

Within the seconds of my death

I said with my very last breath

With their eyes they will see

I was their king to be

Without a Trace

Life filled with misdirection

All truths hidden in the lies

Fallacies lead to a disconnection

This became my demise

It was all just a deception

When can I lose this disguise

I'm never partial to digression

Tears falling from my eyes

This is my final piece of retrospection

As this rhyme ends, my world dies

And all that is left is a collection

Sorry, but these are my last goodbyes

Dread

I understand not where my life is to head

Life no longer synchronous, time merely passing by

My heart is filled with misery and dread

I dare not glance in the mirror

For fear of seeing the darkness and

hatred residing in my eye

Dim

Darkness embraced

Devouring all light and joy

Haunting me with fear

Forever enclosed here

Rot

Do not diminish

The beauty of rotten flesh

Inhale its stench not

For breathless it will leave you

Grave

The foul stench of death

Lingers in the cool night air

Filling hearts with fear

Embraced by a dark abyss

Fright

Behind this door lies

What everyone abhors and denies

Blink . . . one . . . two . . . . they're coming for you

Quick, run down the hall, take a right

Three . . . four . . . you're in for a horrid fright

Don't trip or fall

Five . . . six . . . listen to the demon's call

You can hear the tormenting screams

of those whom fell behind

Seven . . . eight . . . happiness begins to decay

He comes to slay those that locked him away

Nine . . . ten . . . he lurks around the bend

The nightmare will never end

Fool

Every lie you told me

And the fine line you crossed

Should have given away what you were getting in to

But I was too blind to see

That I was becoming lost

And less like me, but more like a fool, more like you

Burning the Skies

Watch me as I burn and die

As the darkness fills the sky

Everyone runs from the night

I awake to spread a terrible fright

Nothing can hold me back

Not even the strong and mighty

The love I had turned tainted and black

They try to hold me down tightly

But the demon inside me tore itself out

Now people only scream and shout

Lullaby for Me

Let me sing you a lullaby

As the stars start to die

Listen closely my dear

Come closer, there is nothing to fear

Drawing my last breath

Dying with the night sky

Give me one last kiss

So I may take leave

With a moment of bliss

Scars and Scratches

These scars that I bear

Will be the last things you see of me

I curl up

And as people walk by

They laugh at me and smile

As the world becomes grim and vile

People will look to me for help

But I'll just say

Get lost you pathetic whelp

River of Blood

Look at the skies and pray

You ran away with my heart

Death is the price you will pay

Blood is to be shed

Fools shall be behead

All life will be drowned in sorrow and dread

As blood runs down my arms like a river

People all around will shiver

Shiver in fear

Crazy

You must be on crack

'Cause this shit is wack

Never look back

Time is what you are starting to lack

Ease and Please

Poems and rhymes come to me with ease.

All I ever do is please. The sounds are sweet.

Hell, I don't even need a bit. Think I'm nothing but weak?

Your future is looking bleak.

Public View

I have quite a few

That one was for public view

Rappers cannot please

I deliver these with ease

Gangsters cower in fright

For I am their nightmare manifest, in day and night

Shadows

As silence and darkness fell

All that was left was an empty shell

You can hear the toll of the bell

And the Shadows, as you can see,

dragged my soul to Hell

Insanity

I'm going insane

And life is getting hard

I have a gun pointed at my brain

Might as well be in a graveyard

This pain

Just won't go away

Precision and Division

Stop there and listen

So I can use the upmost precision

To paint with morbid hues

This is my final decision

With blood red

To fill their heads with dread

Hues that scream

To force upon a morbid dream

And a mutilated human

Barely alive and missing an ear

To fill your dream with fear

No Time

No time for bitches and hos, whores and sluts

I just focus on the pattern of my cuts

Help, I'm stuck in a rut

Feel like a worthless mutt

Don't know if I should jump or not

Bottle of liquor should do the trick

And make me slip

This is the last sip

Now I'm gone, about to hit the ground

Now there is a dead body lying around

Just waiting to be found

Deep Pain

This pain is so deep

I can't help but weep

I need something to dull this pain

You left my heart with a bloody stain

My heart can no longer beat

It was you, who made it obsolete

Can't you see that I can barely stand on my two feet

Dark Abyss / Truest Love

In my mind I keep seeing myself falling to my knees with tears running down my face and my head lifted up as if everything that I had been working on, every beautiful thing I was working on, the one I loved, my family and my friends, were suddenly gone and I was left all alone in this dark abyss where only sorrow and loneliness and depression and fear existed. And that thought, keeps repeating itself, over and over. Until . . . I start to think of you. My truest love and my greatest inspiration.

Hundred Percent

I'm the best

That's a hundred percent possibility

Success is key

You don't even know me

You wish it was me you could be

That's what everyone can clearly see

Small Town

I'm just a small town boy

Who came here from South Detroit

You may think I'm a weird kind of boy

But at least I'm not carrying around a stupid little toy

So everyone jump up with joy

Because I'm bringing this beat all the way back to Illinois

Sold Your Soul

When you sold your soul

You knew you would have to pay this toll

You can keep running til the end of this day

You know you won't be able to get away

I refuse to be what you have made me

I will set myself free

You gave me your hate and you gave me your love

I loathe this fate

You shot me through the heart

And left me to burn

Was it my fault that it was you that I loved

You self-righteous whore

You knew it was you, I could only adore

I'll end it with a razor and lock the door

Flower of Death

Death is in the flower's heart

Why to cry for life of any petal

Death in purple ink of weary pens

Betrays the written yearnings

Upon his paper

Death chuckling at his cries

The broken heart of his

Forlorn upon his sleeve

For Death ignores the plight of any purity

He doth not care or seem to be aware of

What his dreary eyes desired

For Death beckoned unto him

To embrace the vial of dreaded souls

And indeed he did

For no one could love him more

Than what Death did

After all . . . no woman ever would

So Death became his eternal bliss

Phantoms

Dust settles on the floor

Footsteps, unseen and ignored

Marking the path of shadows

That drift in between

As the mettle in a fire's flame

Remains colder than ice

The air is heavy with whispers

That creep past crumbling bones

Shattered glass sparkling in the glass

Daggers to those that look

Into the forbidden walls

Of something that falls

Disintegrating, becoming like ashes

That drift away in the wind

Darkness haunting the hearts of those that stray

Clawing at flesh and bone

Hopelessly crying out

As the fear drives warmth away

Desolate and empty

The walls break away

Joining the broken shards

So the lost and damned

That were forgotten

Are released from their cage and bones

To only be found by those

Who have been driven

By the reek of death

Grim Lies

The light grew dim

My heart turned to stone

Numb, went every limb

Can you not see

That I just want to be left alone

You cannot fathom the amount of

darkness residing within my heart

The scars on my arm

Are from me committing self-harm

When I talk

Not even the Devil can resist my charm

You left me in the cold

You said together we'll grow old

Black turned my loving heart

I used your razor to start

Soul tainted dark and evil

I fall to my knees and weep

As the world becomes dead and grim

The future becomes bleak

Torn Apart

There's nothing for me here

I feel like there is a monster inside me

It wants to rip and tear my heart out

To my knees I collapse

All I can do is scream and shout

As I draw my last breath

The monster inside

Tears itself out

Leading to my miserable death

Hallowed Hearts

There's a party at the beach

Everyone here has a goal to reach

Lift your hands to the sky

And pray that tonight you do not die

Our hearts are hallowed out

Everyone scream and shout

Dance with me in the shroud of night

And let the flames burn high and bright

Watch as phantoms and sirens sing and fly

Bringing our enemies to see this sight

And show them that this is our right

To spread a magnificent fright

Suicide

Gonna die tonight

After I spread a fright

I might slit my wrist

Or shoot myself and leave a list

No one will care

There is nothing more I can bear

Darling Nikki

Darling Nikki rose from the ground

She let out a terrible sound

She turned to me and started to wail

My heart turned cold and frail

In the ground I now lay

It is best to just stay away

Goodbye Baby Goodbye

Goodbye baby goodbye

I never knew what you could feel

I never meant to hurt you or make you cry

I didn't know your pain was so real

Tonight I will make it obsolete

I'll help you stand tall

And lift you off your feet

So you will know, you're better than them all

Blurred Reality

I see nothing but blurs

I can't seem to stop crying

As I look down I see blood

I look at my arms

They're covered in it

I feel faint

I tore out my heart

Love made me hurt

Darkness made me bleed

It's my time to give up

The world will burn

Now I see red

It tells me to rest

The darkness is in my head

Now seeping through my chest

High Delusions

Teens, boys and girls

One night got high

They climbed up on the roof

For they were under

The fatal delusion

That they could fly

One jumped and sadly

The rest followed

While a witness

Stood in terror

Now and forever

Was the witness changed and scarred

Lies All Around

Everywhere there are lies

Spread upon the street

They're on TV

Even in the false, warm faces you meet

Using lies to hide you from bitter truths

None with a real life

Accusing others of false crimes

Slowly killing themselves and their victims

With their own sweet lies

Wrapped in thoughts of lust, gossip, and drugs

They're quickly jumping

Being hung for their foul crimes

A morbid mind

Points onto a nonexistent night

Morbid Dream

I took her down the abyss

And lied her upon a stone slab

And put forth a vicious stab

I mutilated her womb

Now we lay within a tomb

Forever and now

But I'm starting to fade

How can this be, how

It seems love was betrayed

I cry and scream

But it seems there is no awakening

From this morbid dream

Heartbroken

I feel heartbroken

Every time I see you leave

For these words unspoken

I cannot help but grieve

Fearing that time is short

A kiss upon you, I will resort

Lies

I wouldn't know where to begin

Because I've only lied to you once

When I told you

That I would be gone for a couple weeks

Forgive me

I wanted to surprise you

Without You

I want to break down and cry

Because without you I would die

A day without you is like living a nightmare

I want to tell you how I feel

Because with you, I want to be real

But I feel that all I can do is sit and stare

Fear of Rejection

I'm afraid you'll reject me

This fear is infecting me

With thoughts that should not be

Negativity is blinding me

Making me unable to see the truth

Please tell me that it is me you want to be with

Because this isn't the first or second time

I imagined you rejecting me

No, it's more like the fifth

Thoughtless

Was all I did in vain

All of this fear is driving me insane

I'm drawing a blank, scratching at my brain

These thoughts, I cannot refrain

Negative thoughts hit me harder than a train

Images of you

Throwing away my gifts to you and calling them plain

I'm afraid it's you I won't gain

This is my fear, one of the main

Fear One

I fear you find me annoying

Or with my emotions, you're toying

Maybe through Hell, you think we'll be treading

Fear that you think there is no use in trying

Fear that your love for me may be dying

Nevertheless, you will always make my heart

feel like flying

I Don't Want

I don't

Want to be

This guy that

You have no feelings for

I want you

To see me more

Than a friend

For I just can't

Stand not having

You in my life

As my best friend and wife

Scared Of Losing

I'm so scared, so terrified of losing you

That it keeps me from saying what I want

Right now

There is a pain in my heart

Heartache

I feel weird and heartbroken

Maybe because I'm fearing

That your love for me is dying

But I will keep trying

Because there is no denying

My love for you is shining

How Absurd

If you think I don't love you

Do not be absurd

If you want me to

Prove that I love you true

You can take my word

That I will shout it to the world

What Do You Think?

Do you only think of me as a friend? Because that,

I can't stand. If that is all I am. I would collapse to

my knees. I would feel lifeless. And maybe cry.

Because, with you, I was able to fly

Marry Me

My dearest Dayna

All I ask for you tonight

Right here

Right now

You I want to propose to

Marry me and spend

Every moment of our lives together,

forever in serenity

Eternal

Eternal is this love

To grow old with you, would be

Ever so delightful and

Rich in number

Not only did you

Awaken my soul, but also the

Love that lied dormant

Magnificent

May I tell you that in

All my years, never have I seen such

Glorious beauty

Never in a thousand years, could

I ever

Forget one such as you, for

I love you

Countless times I think of you

Every day I wish to see you

Not only to hold you, but

To also kiss and love you

Tranquil

This is the last I need to do

Real are these feelings for you

Am I truly to be

Next to your side

Quietly sitting with you, so

Unique and different

Indeed it is true, this

Love is only for you

Let's Grow Old Together

If I am growing old

Then I want to

Grow old with you

Forever be bold

For the world will behold

Your beauty forever

Shall be told

Forever, forever shall you be

More valuable than gold

Not only to me

But everyone will see

That everlasting is your beauty

Dayna Schwartz

Dayna, my truest love

Allow me to say

You, I wish to marry

Not only do I wish this, but

Also a family with you

Shocking, it must seem

Coming down to saying this

However, this is how I truly feel

Wishing for us to be together, and

Also happy together

Regardless of any misgivings

To you, forever am I devoted

Zach will always be here for you

You

Your voice is all I want to hear

You're all I want to see

Your hands, your lips, your body, and your touch

Are all I want to feel

And you are

The only one I want

The only one I want to spend

The rest of my life with

Night

Never could

I love anyone else

Gladly and forever

Here and always

Til eternity ends, I will love only you

My Darling

My darling Dayna

Listen to what I tell you

I cannot deny

My truest feelings for you

Song For You

A haiku I wrote

To sing for you, my dearest

Giving all my love

To you, my lovely Dayna

Infinite Beauty

Infinite is your beauty

Forever shall it be known

How wondrous and gorgeous

It is you truly are

Your Kiss

Your lips are so full of

Passion, wonder, and bliss

Dayna my love

Please permit me

With innumerable kisses

All About You

Your voice

Full of beauty

Your eyes

Full of fire

Your figure

Full of divinity

Your mind

Full of intellect and knowledge

Your heart

Full of love and wonder

And you lips

So full of passion and bliss

Inspiration

You are my greatest inspiration

To you, my love

Will I show my deepest affection

For you give me a divine sensation

Whenever I am

In your presence

Happy Birthday Dayna

Hello there my love

Aren't you looking fine

Perhaps together we could dine

Poignant is your beauty

You, I wish to be mine

Beauteous and gorgeous Dayna

I must be forthright

Remember what I say tonight

The thing I want to do, is to

Have a long life with you

Dearest Dayna

All these things

You deserve

Darling Dayna

Allow me to tell you that

You light up my world

Not only that, but you

Also make me feel tranquil when I am with you

Expression

So grateful am I, to be able to

Express these feelings to you

Because I now know

You feel the same about me too

Thyne lips

To kiss the lips of thyne

Would be a great pleasure of mine

For truly

You are most fine

Darling of mine

Please give me a sign

I Want

I want to breathe with you

I want to embrace you

I want to kiss you

I want to never let you go

Passionately I would do these things

Only with you

But even more

I want to marry you

And call you mine

Everywhere

Everywhere I look

I hope to see you looking

Looking for me

No one could ever compare to

How it is I see you

Valentine

Venturing onward

As the day sluggishly

Lingers on

Every moment with you

Never could be dull

Think of you constantly

I always do

Never has my heart beat for any other

Everlasting is my love for you

Summer

Such a long time to wait, and it's

Unbearable to think that

Maybe I won't see you again

Maybe you will stop loving me, but

Even if you do

Regardless, I will always love you

Today

Today is a wondrous day

Of course, every day

Dearest Dayna

A glorious one with you

You make every day bright

Stars

Seeing you here

Tonight, makes me feel

As if everything is right

Right now everything is right

So come and hold me tight

Roses Are Red . . .

Roses are red

Violets are blue

A path together with you

Is what I wish to tread

Alone

A day with you

Lovely and darling Dayna

Oh how I love you so

Never could I love any other

Elegance radiates from your very being

Come With Me

Come sit with me

Over by the lone tree

Maybe we can talk

Especially about us

With eternal passion

I pledge to you

To always be faithful

Having love for only you

Me, I pray you choose

Eternally, to be together

Alive

Always with you do I feel

Lively all through the day

Insatiable is this feeling

Vigorously, wishing for you to be mine

Everlasting is thyne beauty

Hands Intertwined

These spaces between my fingers

Are where yours fit perfectly

I close my eyes and think of you

And I reach out to kiss you

I lie awake because I miss you

I wish you were here

By my side

So we can be

Embraced in each other

Don't You Know

Don't you know

Oh don't you know that

Never have I felt

This way before

You light up my world

Only you bring me such joy

Umpteenth is your beauty

Know that I am here for you

Never shall I leave your side

Oath shall I make to thee

Will I forever love you

Infinite Love

My love for you is infinite

And strong

Never does it waiver

In your darkest of times

I will be the light that

Comforts and guides you

The rock that protects you

That shields you from harm

And I shall be the lover

That supports you

And loves only you

Woman

When I drift into slumber

Of you, do I start to dream

More and more, every night

And I daydream about you every day too

Never do I stop thinking of you

Love For You Alone

Not only did I fall

In love with you

I also rose into it

My love is for you

And you alone

Truth is all I speak to you

Because together

I want us to be

And together we will stand

Together we will stand tall

In Love With You

I love you

But I'm not in love

With you

Because if I was

You would be

Reading this right now

Every Moment With You

To spend every waking moment

With you would be

Glorious, and splendid

Is our time together

So much that

I will remember

Remember forever and always

Tonight

This day, March first

Oh how marvelous it is

Not only do I get to see you

I also get to spend time with you

God knows I cherish it

How I cherish it so

Thank you for the memories

Paper To You

It is easier to tell you

How I feel

By writing it to you

Than in person

Because

I fear a rejection

From you

And not some paper

I write on

I Truly Love You

It is oh too easy

To say I love you

To someone you do not

Truly love

But it is incredibly hard

To say those same words

To the person

You are truly in love with

Even harder when you to tell them

That you want to spend

The rest of your life

With them and only them

Which is why

I am always hesitant

To tell you

Dayna

How it is I truly feel

About someone as wondrous

And as beauteous and lovely

As you

So Dayna

I truly love you

Best Days

I do not have a best day in my life

The reason being why

Is that instead

I have many

Many days I declare

To be the best

And the reason why

I have so many

Is because

Many days I have spent with you

And with you

Truly, the days are best

Wedding Bells

As we walk down these halls

Together, hand in hand

And as silence falls

We find ourselves in sand

You can hear the bells toll

From the church

Where we began this beauteous stroll

White Walls

Surrounded by white walls

Standing here together

Everything breaks away and falls

Leaving only the two of us

To exist in this world

To leave you alone

Will I never

Love Of Mine

Love of mine

How ravishing you look

With those lips of thyne

My heart you took

Incased in this book

You will live on in wondrous memory

Kiss Me

Kiss me, Dayna

Kiss me so we may be in our moment of bliss

For this

I surely do miss

Follow Me

Follow my lead

Me and no other

Into the night we go

Our hearts growing stronger

Moments with you are

Of course so full of wonder

Bliss is every moment with you

You, My Dear

You, my dear

Are full of serenity and beauty

My mind cannot fathom

True are my words

Love you, I surely will do

Your Lips

Lips so gentle and soft

Sweeter than any sweets

Than anything delicious

Sugar could never compare

Together

Together with each other

Is what I want to be

Where we need to be

We will always carry on

Belong I do, to only you

Alone With You

Alone with you

With hands intertwined

My heart beats rapidly

True is my love

Love which is only for you

Fire

Forever shall I love you

Into the final days of our lives

Rendering our fears obsolete

Ending them together and standing tall on our feet

Two Hearts Together As One

Our love everlasting

Hearts beat for only each other

Together we will grow old

As time goes on

One moment, we live at a time

Nervous

Nervous to tell you

To tell you everything

Lose the fear we hold

You my love, are my world

Forever In Bliss

Forever in bliss

In this moment we share

Your secrets I shall keep

Embrace me and feel safe

Paradise

Perhaps this is how it should be

Always together

Regardless of what they see

As long as we have each other

Dayna, I promise to you

I promise we will always be

Secure in one another's embrace

Even when you feel alone, I will always be by your side

Everything About You

Your eyes shine brighter than the stars

So much that there seems to be only two

Your smile is like the sun

Bright and beautiful

Your body, like a rose

So gorgeous and thin

Your lips so sweet

Sweeter than sugar

Your hands

Soft like silk

And your embrace

So full of warmth and care

Warmth

What you provide for me is

All I ever needed, and shall I

Return the favor to thee

My lovely Dayna, so full of beauty

Thou art so gorgeous

How lucky am I, to have you in my life

Provide

You provide me with warmth and comfort

You make me smile and laugh

I am prestigious to be in the presence

Of one so beauteous as you

Your voice becalms me

And with this love

I wish to ensnare thee

Every Time

Every time I see you

I want to kiss you

I want to kiss you til day turns to night

I would kiss you every chance I got

If you would permit me please

Four Things

I love you

I miss you

I need you

And I want to marry you

Sweet

Sweet Dayna

Will you be mine?

Every minute we are apart and

Every day I don't see you

These thoughts I have are of you only

Heart Takes Flight

I want to kiss you

And kiss you again

Til night turns to day

And day turns to night

Because with you only

Does my heart take flight

Dayna

Dayna my love

Always shall I love you

You and you alone

Never-ending is your beauty

And everlasting is my love for you

Kiss

Kissing you

Is like

Spending an eternity in

Serenity and bliss

Rose

Remembering every day with you

Oblivious of anyone else

Seeing you everywhere I look

Engulfed within our moment

Passion

Pursuit of your hand

A never pointless quest

Smiling every time I see you

Secretly I wish

I wish you to hold me

Over the short days and long nights

Never will I give up on you

Memory

Memories of you

Everlasting

My love for you lasting

Over the years

Remember what was said

You're here for me and I am here for you

Moments

Moments are

Oh so special

More than we think

Every one with you

Never is a let down

They are instead

So special and meaningful

Los Angeles

Los Angeles

That's your favorite city

Pigeons and all

Someday we'll go

Maybe in the Fall

And we'll see all the sights

Then I'll take you shopping

And then have dinner at the mall

Then finally

I'll take you for a romantic stroll

Precious Moments

Every moment I spend with you

Is more precious than the air I breathe

My heart aches for you

And my lips ache to kiss yours

Future: Won't Give Up

I just won't die

At least not til I tell you

My last goodbye

And give you one last kiss

Because surely, you, I would dearly miss

I Pray

I pray to God to ask him

To put me on the path

Which leads to us

Being together

For the rest of our lives

One Day Of Comfort

I'm glad for one day of comfort, because it might be

the only day all the pain goes away, and I forget all of

my suffering. And I hope and pray, that day is

shared with you.

Wait For You

Forever I'll wait for you

If that's what you need me to do

Forever is how long I will love you too

And to you, I will always be true

Oh Combien Je Vous Adore / Oh How I Adore You

Oh combine je vous adore

Votre beaute eternelle a coup sur

Et pour toujours te supporter

Car tu es magnifique et pure

Avec une allure charmante

Oh how I adore you

Your beauty eternal for sure

And forever you will endure

For you are magnificent and pure

With a charming allure

I Want To Run

Every time I see you

I want to run to you

I want to hold you tight

And I never want to let go

But more importantly

I want to kiss you passionately

Love

Listen my dear, to these words

Overwhelming is your beauty

Valediction has no place here

Every day with you is glorious

Hearts

Here for you always

Even if you don't see me

Always will I be yours

Regardless of what happens

To the end of time

Shall I remain

Woman I Adore

Behind this door

Is a woman I adore

Whom is able to make my heart soar

I shall always love her

Forever and more

Harmonic Melody

Your name is a harmonic melody

So full of beauty

And serenity

Your name outlasting eternity

Forever shall it be

A sweet song to me

The Sweetest Sound

The sweetest sound

I have heard

Was not a mere tune

Or a mere melody

No

It was the sound

The sound of your name

Which beckons to me

The sweetest sound

That ever could be

Dayna

For all eternity

Forever

Forever to always hold

Onto finer days, I've told

Richer than gold

Every spec of beauty

Verified with ever glance

Eternal beauty, has she

Remembered by her glory, forevermore

Beautiful

Beckoning your heart to mine

Everlasting beauty divine

Always waiting for a sign

Undeterred by the laws of time

To kiss the lovely lips of thyne

Into each other, our world define

Full of your beauty, shall intertwine

Uncountable acts of love

Losing our sense of time

Only You

Oh my love

Not only do you give me light

Love is also what you give

Yearning to be with you

You alone make the day bright

Oh how I love thee

Unconditionally for eternity

What Is

Oh my darling

What is life

Life is love

What is love

Love is kissing

What is kissing

Come here and I shall show you

Comfortable With Waiting

I feel comfortable for you and with you

The thought of losing you and not having you

Scares me

And if I ever did

I believe I would die

Thank You

Thank you for all the things you have done.

Our time together was fun. To me, you are sweeter than

honey. You always made me laugh and smile.

You were always very funny. With you, I'd walk an

eternal mile. Thank you for making me smile.

Be Mine

Before I met you

Everything was mundane

Majestic and beautiful

I love everything about you

Never will I forsake you

Everlasting is your beauty

Didn't Want To Let Go

After you told me, "I love you"

I didn't want to let you go

Yet I couldn't tell you

For I was too slow

I wish for another kiss

So I may be, again, in bliss

Caught Off Guard

You caught me off guard

With the kiss you gave me

I was slow to react

That's because I felt like I was in a dream

It was a moment of bliss

One I wish to have again

Loving Embrace

I want to hold your hand

I want to kiss your lips

And make you feel grand

With my hands on your hips

And your arms around my neck

Both of us together

In loving embrace

Love Is Not Blind

Some say love is blind

But true love with you, is what I find

How could I possibly be blind

If I can see you perfectly

So now, without fear and hesitation holding me back

I must declare my love for you

Or lose you to the fear and be a fool

Dream Come True

To be alone with you

Is like a dream come true

To love only you

Is all I care to do

My Angel

My angel, my darling

Never let me go, I beg you please

Only for you, will my heart sing

Wanting to kiss you and kiss you again

My love for you will never cease

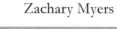
Kiss Your . . .

Kiss your neck

Kiss your cheek

Kiss your head

Kiss thyne lips

Place my hands on your hips

Lead me to your bed

You are what I seek

I gladly give a kiss, not a peck

Kiss Me, Kiss Me Again

Kiss me, kiss me again

And tell me you will be mine

My perfect little valentine

And forever with me, remain

You Gave . . .

You gave me light

And you gave me love

You gave me laughter and a smile

You raised me up when I was down

And you brought my heart to its knees

Give me your hand, will you please

Ces Nuits Sans Toi A Mes / These Nights Without You

Ces nuits sans toi a mes cotes sont insupportables

Envie de vous pour etre avec moi

Ma Cherie, Je t'aime

J'espere que tu m'aimes aussi

These nights without you by my side are unbearable

Desiring you to be here with me

My darling, I love you

I hope that you love me too

What Does My Heart Do Around You

My heart races when I see you

And it skips when I am with you

And when you talk to me, it soars

And when you look back at me with love, it flies

But when you kiss me, it falls back down

Only to be with yours in turn

Focused

You're so focused that it makes me smile

So beautiful in your studies

Your fashion of lovely style

Your eyes more gorgeous than the seas

With you, I'd walk an eternal mile

So we may one day, carve our names into trees

Days Without You

These days without you are long

Yet whenever I catch a glimpse of you

Not only does my heart race

It also grows strong

You always manage to take my breath away

Always will you look stunning

And together we belong

I Need You

Your beautiful locks of hair

Are pleasant to the sight

And so lovely and fair

The shine from your heavenly light

Is more than I can bear

I wish you to hold me tight

Because the only thing I am able to do, is stare

I need you to tell me everything will be alright

I want you to stay with me

A special promise, I will make to you

Together we will always be

Forever will my love for you be true

Intertwined is our fate

A kiss from your lips

Would truly be great

Your hand on my cheek

And min on your hips

You're so beautiful you gleam

You are my beautiful dream

I Shall Tend

When you are injured

I shall tend to your wounds

When you are hungry

I shall make sure you are fed

When you are tired

I shall let you rest

And when you feel alone

I shall remain by your side

Change

Change is good

But it is better

When things change with you and the one you truly love

I wish for us to always be together

Regardless of the things that change around us

But one thing that will never change

Is my everlasting love for you

All I Ever Want

All I ever want to be

Is with you

Whether it be alone

Or surrounded with friends

For when I am with you

I feel grand

Together we will never fall

But firmly stand

Beautiful Day

It's always a beautiful day

With you around

Everything is calm and sweet

I would gladly kiss you

And sweep you off of your feet

If you would permit me

And tell you, you fill me with glee

Stay With Me

Sometimes I like

These poems do you no justice

And they aren't worth the effort

Yet, you say they're incredible

What I wouldn't give to see

Into our future

To hold you and call you mine

Having you with me

Making me feel blissful

Every time we are together

Ignorant Fool

I swallow my pride

And push all this useless negativity aside

Because when I see you

You walk with a graceful stride

Never could I lie to you

That's just one of the many things I could never do

For if I did

I would be an ignorant fool

Night And Day

To my knees I collapse

I feel like time is about to relapse

If I don't get what I'm feeling off my chest

With you I can find peace and rest

Til the end of my life

I pray you'll be my wife

To you, I will only say

I find comfort and joy with you, night and day

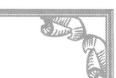

Can't Fall

It doesn't matter if my legs are on the verge of giving out or not. I'll just keep running to you, I won't ever stop. Never will I give up, your love is like an adrenaline shot. With you by my side, we'll both stand tall. And we'll tear down these barriers, this demeaning wall. With you, I can't possibly fall.

Running Out Of Time?

I have an aspiration to complete this rhyme

Because I want to tell you what I'm really feeling

I might be running out of time

So here are the cards I'm dealing

A life without you, doesn't seem real

I love you and that's the way I truly feel

The Thing I Desire

The way you look is glorious

And the way you feel is lovely

Your figure is delightful and gorgeous

Your beauty fills the moon with jealousy

The thing I desire most, is your hand in marriage

And your everlasting and unconditional love

Let Us Prove Them Wrong

Many say that nothing lasts forever

But I aim to prove them wrong

My love and admiration for you knows no bounds

Your voice is indeed, the loveliest of sounds

Our times together are all I care to remember

Together with each other

Is where we belong

Plans And Hopes

You're so full of beauty

It brings me joy

To see someone as gorgeous as you

Is a gift I dare not take for granted

You are the love of my life

What I plan and hope to do

Is marry you

Shine So Bright

You shine so bright throughout the night with an

outstanding light. Your beauty is shines brilliantly.

Your body, to see, is a wondrous sight. How glorious it is

to see you and even more, to be with you.

True Beauty

Lips sweeter than sugar

Figure most divine

Eyes more beautiful than the ocean after a storm

Smile brighter than the sun

Voice lovelier than a siren song

Laugh so beautiful

Nose cuter than a button

Skin like snow

Hair sexy as can be

The true beauty of her, you can truly see

Forever Together, Together Forever

Aquarius and Pisces are forever together

Just like Romeo and Juliet

That's how I want us to be

Always together, forever

My Love

My love, I have tried with all my being

To grasp a form comparable to thyne own

But nothing seems worthy

I know now, why Shakespeare could not compare

his love to a summer's day

It would be a crime to denounce the beauty of such

a creature as thee

To simply cast away the precision God had

placed in forging you

Each facet of your being

Whether it physical or spiritual

Is an ensnarement from which there is no release

But I do not wish release

I wish to stay entrapped forever

With you for all eternity

Our hearts, always as one

My Vow To You

When you are sad, I will dry your tears

When you are scared, I will comfort you

When you need love, my heart I will share

When you are sick, for you I will care

You will feel my love when we are apart

Knowing that nothing will change my heart

When you are worried, I will give you hope

When you are confused, I will help you cope

When you are lost and cannot see the light

My love will be a beacon, shining ever so bright

This is my vow to you, one I pledge til the end of eternity

For you above all, are my wife and best friend

These words I have written

Speak of my love for you

From my lips, these words spoken

Shall always ring true

God has blessed me

And with your hand in mine

Both of our hearts

Will forever intertwine

Happy In Marriage

Into all lives, falls pain and sorrows

I promise together, we will meet all tomorrows

Happy in marriage, honor, and love

Blessed in unity, by God above

Darling Of Mine, Give Me A Sign

Darling of mine

You make the world shine

You are sexy and fine

Whenever you're around, my heart rate inclines

Will you give me a sign

To let me know, that you are willing to be mine

Lullaby For You

This lullaby, I sing for you

You gave me the strength to make this perfect

Only for you, this I would do

Never think yourself a defect

Truth is, you're flawless

And a beautiful woman

Yet, you're more like a goddess

Your brilliance shines so bright

That not even the moon can withstand the sight

I Promise

I promise to always be faithful to you

And to wipe away all the tears you shed too

I will always love you

Forever and true

You are my world and true love

And I promise to always stand by your side and

protect you too

I love you

Love

With this rose, I not only give you merely a rose,

but I give you my heart and souls. I send to you,

all the love I have to give, and anything else that

would give me the chance to touch your heart.

With this rose, I reveal all my thoughts and

feelings about you that I have withheld for so

long. I feel when I am with you . . . I am like a

rose. Not because of its beauty, no, but because

I am able to bloom and grow with you. To me,

you are like a rose's sunshine. So full of energy

and light, that never does it fail to lift my spirits.

Just by the sound of your voice and that look

in your eye. I could never tear my eyes away

from you; you are able to make my life worth living. But, without you, just like a rose, I would wither and die. Not all at once, but little by little, petal by petal. Slowly at first, because you have made me stronger and stronger each day you're with me. But eventually, without you, I will lose all of those beautiful you have given me.

Through Thick And Thin

Dayna, you're beautiful and lovely

And I vow to always be here for you

Through thick and thin

To marry and spend my whole life with you

Is what I plan to do

Will you accept me, a humble fool?

Bewitched

I stare into your eyes

And I feel bewitched

How someone as beautiful as you

Could ever love me

I cannot comprehend

I never want to let you go

My deepest love for you I want to show

When I am with you, my heart doesn't just race, it flies

I want to keep you in my sight

And be with you, day and night

To Be With You

I desire to be with you

Til the end of our days, til the end of eternity

You are my angel

My heart burns with passion

You complete me

And I wish to complete you as well

Three Words

These three words are often said, but hold no

meaning. But to me, when I say them to you, they

mean the world. As you mean the world to me.

I hope that you can see, that all I ever want to be, is

with you. I hope these three words; show you that

you are more precious to me than

diamonds and air. To me, you are beautiful

and flawless. And the three words I

want to tell you are . . . I love you

Dayna

Her eyes, the beautiful color of sage

Her brilliance that is no fallacy

Fills the moon with a jealous rage

She's like something out of a fantasy

Her figure is lovelier than that of a rose

She brings happiness and joy wherever she goes

Skin white as snow

She radiates with a loving glow

She's brighter than the stars

And her smile, brightens my world

If I Lost You

If I lost you, I wouldn't be able to go on

You're the one who made me strong

I wouldn't be able to accept that you were gone

I just wouldn't be able to move one, I would think that

It would be just wrong

The love you showed for me and the love

I showed for you

We go hand in hand

We'll stay together forever, and together,

we'll firmly stand

Without You, The Day Is Dull

The day is dull without you

The sun rises just to see your beauty

The moon sets to hide its shame

You, I wish for myself to claim

Loving you will be my eternal duty

For I can only love one such as you

Risking Sounding Like A Fool

I'm risking sounding like a fool

I made you a story

I did this for you

Not the fame and glory

These feelings for you, I can no longer conceal

For you I will be honest and real

So now I must tell you

I love you

Love Is Sweet

Love is sweet

Love is kind

As our lips meet

Our hearts become strong

I see the fire in your eyes

The love never dies

How Can I Not

How can I not love someone such as you

You are in every way, beautiful

What I really want, is to be with you

I love you and I hope you love me too

Every time I think of you, my heart races

I cannot imagine my life without you

My heart belongs to you and you alone

You are gorgeous and fine

Won't you say, you'll be mine?

Representation

A rose represents beauty

Sweets represent kindness

You are more beautiful than a rose

Such that, it is undeserving

To even be compared to you

Your kindness is sweeter than any kind of sweet

Your figure is divine

Even more divine than that of a rose

I wish to be with you, for eternity

Constantly, I Think Of Only Her

All I ever do is think

I think of her constantly

I love her and hope she loves me

I am like a rose

I need her like a rose needs the sun

She brightens my day and gives me energy

Without her I would wither away

I want and need to be with her

With me, I hope and pray she stays

If Beauty had A sound

If beauty had a sound. I can only fathom that
it would be your name being said. You erased
my sorrow and dread. You gave me hope and
love. You raised me up above all the rest. And
now, you give me a place to rest my weary head.
Right next to yours. In this warm, caring bed.

If Roses Did Not Exist

If doses did not exist

You would surely take their place

They wouldn't ever be missed

For there is much more beauty in your figure alone

You're gorgeous and beautiful

I beg you not to change

You are my world

My everything

Every day we are apart

My heart aches

Talking to you makes my heart soar

You, I only adore

When I dream

I dream of an angel

An angel that is you

When I think

I think of only you

You are indeed fine

I truly love you

And I pray, that you will be mine

Will you accept me, a fool?

You Are My World, Dayna

You my love, are my world

Your eyes are like the stars

Your smile is like the sun

Always bringing light into my world

Your beauty is like the moon

Always brilliant and visible

You make the darkness in my world obsolete

Always to you I shall be true

For indeed it is true that

I love you

You Are The One For Me

You made my heart melt so easily

I didn't understand how

I was blind and could not see

When I am not with you

I want to cry

I now know the reason why

You always make my heart fly

Without you, I would die

And now I see

You are the one for me

Hello Beautiful

Hello beautiful

Did you know that I love you

I think of you constantly

And I will do anything that will make you happy

Your beautiful emerald eyes have captured me

Some say love is blind

But clearly I can see

You are the love of my life

They say that true beauty comes from within

I have not seen true beauty, until I saw you

Hopefully, your heart I can win

Your figure is divine

All I want is you

Will you accept me, a humble fool?

Blue Rose

Rose. Rose. Ever seen a blue rose? They're different and beautiful. Just like you. Many say they don't exist. They say it because they hate difference. Why are they so cruel? Are they scared? Or just too ignorant to accept difference? Those poor fools. Not a kind heart amongst them.

My Heart Sings

Joy she brings. Always and only for her, my heart sings. I'm addicted to this happiness you brought me. I never want it to go away. With you, I always want to be. Hopefully your heart I will win and with me you will stay. Tonight I declare my love for you. For if I don't, I fear I would lose you and feel a fool.

I Shall Wait

Not only do I love you

I also adore you too

I'll wait til you're ready

Because with you, I'll go steady

The Rest of My Life

I finally found out

What I want to do

With my life

Spend the rest of it

With you

Saturday . . .

As Saturday draws near

Not seeing you for days or ever again

Is my worst fear

My faith, however, stays

For you, I shall be strong

Your name, a beautiful song

Dreaming

I fantasize and dream about you

Not only did I fall in love with you

But I also rose into it

Forgive me for seeming like a fool

But without you, I wouldn't know what to do

You are my muse

And for you, I'd gladly pay these dues

Dayna I Love You

Dreaming to one day call you mine
All I really want is you
You are my world, my everything
No matter what happens
Always shall I love and care for you

I have never seen true beauty

Least, not til I met you
Only I can say what true beauty looks like
Very lovely and intelligent, you are
Everlasting is your beauty

Yearning to be with you
Only you, I can love
Unconditionally, til the end of my days

Her Lovely Kiss

Her lovely kiss

Always full of bliss

Surely I do miss

Desire to give her this

A life together

Always and forever

Quote

I love you

But I'm not in love with you

If I was

You would be reading this

Right now

True Feelings

The way I truly feel about you . . .
Every day I am not with you, fills me with sorrow.
I think of you constantly. My love for you is
true and everlasting, as is your beauty. I want
and I need to spend the rest of my days with
you. Because I want to have a long and happy
life with you. It may seem foolish of me to say,
that you are the one for me, and I hope and
pray, that I am the one for you. You always make
me smile. And if I don't have you, I would be
nothing. I will always love you unconditionally
and wipe away every tear that you shed. You are
my world. Dayna, you are my true love and the
love of my life. I love you, forever and always.

I Fear This

Dayna, let me tell you the things in which I fear

I fear losing you and becoming someone you don't

want to deal with

I fear never seeing you again or being able

to call you mine

What I am hoping for, is a sign

A sign from you

To show me, that you will always be mine

I'm Risking It

Risking sounding like a fool

I raise my head to the sky

And my mind races to you

These feelings for you

I cannot deny

When I talk to you

My heart skips

And when I am with you

It races

How badly I wish

To kiss your magnificent lips

You erase my mind of doubts

Even in the darkest of places

Happiness is what you bring

My heart overflows with delight

I can't help but sing

You bring my heart to its knees

And in this dull, dark world

You always make it shine bright

Sweet And Tender

Your lips are so sweet and tender

And your figure is gorgeous and slender

Your skin is soft and fine

Your smile makes the world shine

You're beautiful and lovely

My darling, I wish you to be mine

I love you, always and true

I Would Only Whisper

If I had to

Scream to the world

That I love you

I would only whisper

Whisper it to you

Because you

Are my world

My Words Are Only True

May words may be sweet

But not as sweet as thyne lips

Your beauty is unmatched

Your smile lights up my world

Your eyes are more beautiful than the ocean

Your figure is even more divine than that of a rose

Your beauty is never ending

As is my love for you

Kiss You Again

Your lips I wish to kiss

Again, so I may be in our moment of bliss

Being by your side

I surely do miss

Forgive me for saying this

But I want to marry you

Sorry if I seem a fool

Forever with you, is what

I wish the future to lead to

Rest Of My Life

I long to kiss your lips

So tender and sweet

I want to place my hands on your hips

And lift you off your feet

You are truly a delightful sight

I want and I need

To spend the rest of my life with you

Day and night

Dayna Rose Schwartz

Dearest Dayna

Always shall I love you

You are my true love

Never could I feel the same towards anyone else

All of this time to wait

Reminds me of all the glorious times we spent together

Of course we seem to be

Strangers to each other, but

Even that won't stop me

Stop me from loving you, it will not

Come with me and you will see

How much I truly do

Want to spend the rest of my life with you

And not only that, but you will see

Regardless, I will love you with a fierce intensity

Til the end of my days and til the end of eternity

Zach, will always feel the same towards you

For You

Most of these poems are about you

It's all I really care to do

But what I would care to do more of

Is spend time with you

Even if it's minutes, or few

Because, I only love you

And I wish to know you

You

My heart is racing

Faster and faster it goes

An image of you

My mind shows

Capable, you are of

Leaving me breathless

My dear . . .

I cannot take this

I need to know

I need to see you

I need to hold you

I need to talk to you

I need to kiss you

And I need to love you

You are

My true love

My greatest inspiration

I fear losing you

I fear to not have you in my life

I fear not being able to call you mine

I fear not winning your love

Not winning your heart and affection

I fear not winning your hand in marriage

Forever

Shall my words ring true

Never a lie be told

I want to hold you

I want to hold your hand

I want to know you

I want to see you

I want to speak with you

I want to kiss you

I want to love you

I want your hand in marriage

I only love you

Forever and always

I can only love you, Dayna